Today and Other Seasons

Today and Other Seasons

Poems by

Sarah Russell

Cover design by Shay Culligan:

Cover art "Bountiful" by Elena Nosyreva
www.elena-nosyreva.pixels.com

ISBN: 978-1-952326-01-1

Kelsay Books
502 South 1040 East, A-119
American Fork, Utah 84003

For my 96-year-old mother-in-law,
Boby Clariana
who likes my poetry even though it doesn't rhyme

~

With thanks to Roy Clariana
for his love and support

~

and to
Timmy Shanahan, Ryan Stone,
and Steve Deutsch for their help
with early drafts of this chapbook

~

Acknowledgments

Eclectica: Near Jack's Cabin

Ekphrastic Review: Montana Man, Reaping

Loyalhanna Review: Green Tomato Chutney, Opening Day,
    Age 12

Pastiche: Summer Wash Day, 1952

Prey Tell: Winter Hawk, republished in *Poetry Nook*
    (honorable mention)

Red Eft: Backroads

The Houseboat: Migrating Geese, republished in *Poems for the*

Waiting Room: Petrichor, September, Starlings

Word Fountain: November Doe

Your Daily Poem: Cusp, Dandelions, High, In April,
    Metamorphosis, Nesting

Contents

Today

a child skips toward tomorrow.
An elder yearns for yesterday.
Mid-life careens through moments,
not even aware of its breath.

Somewhere a dove mourns
for a scatter of feathers
in the grass.

Cusp

Yesterday's south wind rushed warmth
to February snow. Today the earth
is boggy with new grass, tattered white
in crannies on north sides of things.
Daffodils finger their way toward light,
and old women's feet no longer tremble
on their way to market.

The early March calf

struggles to stand in heavy snow
at the seam where meadow meets woods.
Its mother laps the afterbirth, while coyotes,
skeletal from winter, circle, silent as smoke.
The cow bellows, charges the snarling wraiths.
I run to help, yell, wave my arms, watch
their shadows disappear in scruff beyond the fence.
The mother turns to look my way, then urges
her calf toward the herd, away from carnivores.

In April

I wake to birds calling to spring
and rain, slow and steady,
nudging the tulips. In the gray
of my morning walk, forsythia
create moments of sunshine
against the monotone of clouds—
blossoms tumbling down the hillside
like children laughing.

Metamorphosis

Heavy spring snow overnight,
more than predicted, slush
on the path, cotton-laden branches,
bewildered robins. It is sudden
and white, everything white,
erasing April. By evening the sun
will wave its warmth like a wand
and spring will reappear, but oh,
the beauty of a whitewashed field,
my dark footprints, my dog's nose-down,
meandering delight.

Opening Day, Age 12

For my cousin John Russell

The ritual started days before—
finding Grandpa's fly rod
in its frayed canvas case
and the reel, handled so the sheen,
once green as summer oaks,
was worn away. Dad gave them
to me after Grandpa died, and I cried
all over again. I got out the old book
that showed how to tie the knot between
line and leader, leader and hook,
remembered Grandpa's tobacco breath,
close, as he showed me that first time.

The night before, I dug for worms, stored
them in a soup can by the wicker creel
that smelled of grass and brook trout
Grandpa'd caught for supper. "Don't let them
suffer," he said. "They're too pretty to suffer,"
and he'd snap their necks and gut them there
on the bank with the knife he got as a boy.
My knife now.

At first light, I left the house, careful
the screen door didn't bang, and hiked
across the field where horses silhouette
dark in the mist. The creel on its worn strap
banged my hip, my arms gooseflesh in the dawn.
The stream spoke as I neared, and I tiptoed
on the grassy bank. "Fish scatter if they feel
a tremble," Grandpa said. "They can hear you too,"
he whispered.

There's a place he showed me
where the "big one" lived—the one Grandpa
never caught, though he got close a time or two.
I set the creel down in the willows, fuzzy
with pollen, and looked into the shadows
where the bank cut deep. This wasn't the sport
of men in waders, the swish and snap of lines cast
to a river's flow. Instead I baited the hook
and let the leader plop upstream to drift. I heard
my breath, the hum of a dragonfly, and Grandpa
whispering, "Good."

Nesting

The finches are courting
outside our window, a warbled
discussion of real estate and love.
Like last year and the year before,
they want to lease the flower wreath
on our front door. It's always a dilemma—
discourage their rapture or detour
through the garage?

The finches always win. So for a month,
we'll wake to overtures at dawn—so cheerful,
so loud—show pictures of pin-feathered babies
to friends, recall demands and pleasures
of our own brood, the bittersweet fledging.

In Amish country

based on "The Team,"
a painting by Florence Cichocki

six horses,
sometimes twelve,
plow spring fields.
Farmers guide with whistles,
clucks and sweat-soaked reins,
their shirts echoing the sky.
Earth receives the blade,
sighs her musky scent,
reveals hidden stones
and the sinew of old roots.
Sowing will follow
if the rain holds off
a day or two.

Dandelions

Spike-haired, brass-blonde,
they invade the bluegrass suburbs
where blades form a passive sameness
if tended as intended. They strut
across the green of every day—
strumpets in tattered leafy skirts,
stiletto roots—bestowing downy favors
on the summer breeze.

Summer Wash Day, 1952

Mondays,
we wheeled the wringer washer,
mule stubborn, squeaking protest
from its tiny wheels (dowager
on a dance floor) to the kitchen sink,
attached a hose to fill the tub,
added soap and plugged it in.

Whites were first, slosh sloshing,
soap tumbling over tub top,
as rhythm danced our lady
across the stained wood floor.
Wringing was the hard part.
My sister cranked the handle,
I fed dripping sheets and towels,
kept fingers from harm's way.
Then another load to slosh,
before the tub refilled to rinse
and wring again. Finally, baskets
heaped and heavy, we headed
for the yard, wooden clothes pegs
pocketed in cobbler aprons.

There's an etiquette to hanging wash.
We stretched to pin the tops of sheets,
shoulders of shirts, waists of pants,
underwear hung modestly on inner lines.
We slid the clothes pegs into place
and made sure things were hanging straight
so neighbors didn't talk. Then we propped
a tall, forked stick midway when a line
was full to lift it high to catch the breeze.

Clothes dried stiff, sun-bleached,
were folded as we took them down,
brushing bugs and leaves away.
But if it rained, we ran to grab things
willy-nilly, laughing, squealing, drops
spattering our arms and faces.

At night we burrowed deep
in our beds, nuzzling the smell
of sunshine caught in cotton.

Roller Skating

We clamped them on our saddle shoes
with skate keys, buckled leather straps
around our ankles, clattered metal wheels
down pebbled sidewalks past the Borgman's
and the Shaw's and that rental no one mowed.
Old Miz Yonkers's driveway was the best—
smooth and two cars wide! We sailed
on that unpebbled course, arms flailing,
skinned knees and elbows orange with iodine,
tattered bandaids barely hanging on.

High

The slat seat solid under me,
I push off, lean back, hands tight
around the chains, sail forward,
find the rhythm. Legs pump
until the schoolyard and the sky's a blur
of clouds and asphalt, until my stomach
gives a little flip, hairs on my arms
tingle, and the still summer air's
a breeze.

Uncle Dell's Barbershop

smelled of Bay Rum and soap.
A 12-point trophy buck glowered
from the wall. There were tattered
Field and Streams and a table-sized
cribbage board where stakes
were a penny a point.

Uncle Dell taught me to play,
sharpened my strategies.
When I turned twelve, he pitted me
against the men, told them to throw me
one good crib and then watch out.
Oh, my grin of triumph if I won,
when they harrumphed and paid up
while he snipped and winked my way.

I'd take my winnings to the drugstore,
order a double-dip,
sashay home.

Backroads

A mosaic of grime blurs the view
through the only window left whole
on this homestead, abandoned to vermin
and weeds grown leggy through the floor.
The fields beyond cast matte pastels
of wheat, barley, sky. In a bedroom
I find a rag doll missing an arm. I cradle her,
feel the ache of mule-pulled plows,
drought-bleached days.

Petrichor

Start with a kiln-dry summer day,
when the earth cracks with longing,
and sweat makes tracks between your breasts.

The air's so still you hear a beetle scuttle
on the screen, the sun dims in a sullen sky,
and crickets stop chirping.

Then it starts—the first lazy drops—

and when the porch step's dappled,
lift your face to the embrace and breathe in
the mix of dust and rain like a lover's musk.

Starlings

There's a sash of clouds slung low along the ridge
and a blur of rain in the valley. An abacus
of starlings perch on the telephone lines
adding and subtracting. Suddenly they lift—
a single, peppered swirl dipping left, then right
as wings astound the sky.

Reaping

based on "Arles: View from the Wheat Fields"
a painting by Vincent Van Gogh

It is a good year, a good harvest—
the wheat, gold as a king's coins,
as a lover's hair freed from her combs.
At sunset, when the sky turns gold
we are gilded too—our skin
becomes the sheaves—the ache of bending,
of swinging the scythe, of gathering,
forgotten.

September

Black-eyed Susans gossip in a gully
between the road and corn past harvest,
clouds in feather boas waltz through pale
silk skies, and cows head home for milking.

The hawk holds vigil on a fence post.

In Passing

Autumn eases us from summer's excess—
the exuberance of annuals, the castanet
of crickets. Trees ignite, then bid farewell
to leaves playing hopscotch on the wind.
The sweaters we pull close whisper of cider
and home games, patchwork trails, and earth,
redolent with dying. We chop wood
and hang rosemary to dry, knowing November
will need them through its barren waiting.

Green Tomato Chutney

Each fall (always by serendipity)
I find green tomatoes at the farmer's market.
I could order them, of course, from the Amish
in the last stall on the left, but that would take away
the magic.

Picked hastily before first frost, they nestle
with the Brandywines and Early Boys and take me
by surprise. I smile, my weekend planned, and buy
six pounds. Come Saturday, I'll make chutney.

Then another sortie through the stalls. Everything
must be fresh picked—peppers, patent leather red,
rose-streaked Gala apples, chubby garlic bulbs,
currants round as BBs, bunioned ginger toes
and raisins, withered gold.

My basement yields an oddment of jars
and the large blue pot that waits for this occasion.
I whet my favorite knife, find cutting boards
and colanders, and blues on the radio. The tunes
remind me of hard times, when canning meant
peach jam at Christmas, and women wore aprons.

I put mine on (a gift from my husband
before he knew better), wash vegetables,
and start to work. I pare and core and chop
and mince, humming with Muddy Waters,
Bessie Smith, peeling the next apple,
and the next.

The blue pot's almost full—a kaleidoscope
of harvest. Next comes sugar, tawny with molasses,
then spices—cumin, cinnamon, cayenne, sea salt,
nutmeg, cloves. I add malt vinegar and set the blue pot
on the stove.

Chutney needs its own heat—too high will scorch
a day's work; too low, and it will turn to mush.
I set the flame just so, and change the music—
now conjuring a sultan's rapture, for soon aromas
like a dance of veils, exotic as Tangiers, whisper
secrets of the oda.

I wash the jars, dry them on white linen towels,
put water in a roasting pan to boil, once more
attend the chutney—stirring as the liquid turns
to syrup, raisins plump, and currants soften.

Alchemy achieved, at last the chutney's ladled into jars
and bathed—a purifying rite. The blue pot's washed,
its task complete. The jars come out with tongs to rest
again on linen towels—three rows of five to give to friends
and bring the Silk Road to our table.

I pour a cup of tea, listen for the soft, inverse pop, pop
of lids sealing in the fantasies.

Migrating Geese

Keening in a bruised sky,
ragged chevrons
follow the coastline south—
imperfect V's, left wanting
on one side or the other—
testament, perhaps, to those taken
by foxes, hunger, double barrels,

their skeins unraveling autumn.

November Doe

The twitch of an ear betrays her,
dun against dun oaks, still as held breath.
How long has she watched me?
I look beyond for others, but she's alone,
fat from summer grazing, her coat
already wooly for January snows.
The morning is alive, anticipating flight
as she moves, slow, along the scruff
of goldenrod that marks the meadow,
then turns back to the woods and disappears,
asking no questions.

Montana Man

based on "End of Autumn,"
a photograph by Todd Klassy

He squints from under a John Deere cap
even when there is no sun. It's late fall now,
the hay, enough this year, baled for January
feeding if the pickup makes it to the herd—
huddled, wooly, steamy breath to match his own,
pitch fork separating clouds of gold, strewing it
like a Silver Wolf high roller—that kind of pride,
though pride's a wobbly perch when drought
and blight's the norm, when the pickup
needs a fuel pump, barn needs shingles.

But today, the sky is wide and blue and bare,
and Waylon's singing "Ramblin' Man"
while he hums along. Bernice'll have coffee
scalding hot at the cafe, and prices were up
on the farm report this morning. Folks and steers
aren't so different, he reckons, herd gathering,
keeping with their kind.

New England Winter

Old timers call it bracing, keep flasks
in back pockets. They smack gloved hands
together in the general store, stomp snow
off while their fellows yell to dammit,
shut the door. They speak of worse winters—
remember '63? And '96 when drifts were high
as the Lutheran Church and you couldn't stay
ahead of it, it came so fast. Hell, they say,
this ain't so bad, and spit tobacco juice. Specks
of it sizzle on the stove, and Old Man Pettigrew
behind the counter yells to dammit, aim better.

January Nehi

Just off the highway at a country store,
the customer before me bought a Nehi grape soda
in a tall, scuffed bottle, and suddenly I was eight again,
cold sweetness coloring my tongue, the bottle sweaty
in my hand, summer just starting. So I said, "Just a sec,"
to the woman at the counter and got one from the cooler.
"Haven't had one in years," I told her.

"You want it uncapped?"

"I forgot that part," I said as she produced a church key
on a grubby string. I drove on through snow-draped hills,
smoke rising from wood stoves in the valley, swigging
luscious, fizzy purple, skipping barefoot in my mind.

Winter Hawk

Silent sentry in a ravaged tree,
his fields, once tall with corn,
now snow-tipped stubble.

He accepts the unforgiving wind,
the cold, thin light—not wishing
for tomorrow or warmth or spring—
alive only in what is.

Suddenly he rises on fierce,
decisive wings—his crimson tail
as brilliant in the January sky
as truth.

Near Jack's Cabin

deer . . . like skeletons.
—Dorothy Wordsworth

Yes, like skeletons this winter,
stealing silage meant for cattle
though it starves them.
They look wistful at the forest's edge.
I want to coax them to my fire
before the wind tonight and snow,
more snow.

Some will fawn in spring if they survive.
We shall shrug off matted coats,
browse among the daffodils.

About the Author

Sarah Russell has returned to poetry after a career teaching, writing, and editing academic prose. She holds an M.A. in Mass Communication from the University of Denver and a Ph.D. in Communication Theory from the University of Colorado. Her poems have been published in *Kentucky Review, Red River Review, Misfit Magazine, Third Wednesday, Psaltery and Lyre,* and many other journals and anthologies. She has awards from Goodreads, Poetry Nook, and is a Pushcart Prize nominee. Her first poetry collection *I lost summer somewhere,* was published by Kelsay Books in 2019. She lives in State College, Pennsylvania, with her husband Roy Clariana. They spend summers in Colorado to be near children and grandchildren. She blogs at SarahRussellPoetry.net.